MW01068325

THE KEEPER

*Surviving Dark Places
In the Light of His Grace*

LISA M. MANASCO

Library of Congress Cataloging-in-Publication Data

ISBN: 978-1-5439-9639-5 (hardcover)
ISBN: 978-1-54399-640-1 (ebook)

Printed in the United States of America.

"I will lift up my eyes to the hills—from whence comes my help?

My help comes from the Lord who made heaven and earth.

He will not allow your foot to be moved; He who keeps you will not slumber.

Behold, He who keeps Israel shall neither slumber nor sleep.

The Lord is your keeper; The Lord is your shade at your right hand.

The sun shall not strike you by day, nor the moon by night.

The Lord shall preserve you from all evil; He shall preserve your soul.

The Lord shall preserve your going out and your coming in from this time forth, and even forevermore."

—PSALM 121:1-8

"*The Keeper*, the Lisa Manasco story, pulls no punches. This is a must read! In spite of what life has dealt her, she found the courage to persevere, the courage to forgive, and the courage to make choices that reflected an unwavering faith in God. Today Lisa thrives in the light of God's grace."

DWIGHT THOMPSON, EVANGELIST
DWIGHT THOMPSON MINISTRIES

"Are you ready to start a new chapter in your life? How your life begins does not determine how it ends. You can recreate your life story any time you choose to, and Lisa Manasco is proof. In her first book, she takes you on the unimaginable personal journey of experiencing extreme hopelessness, fear and the tragedy of losing nearly every single member of her family.

"Lisa is proof that the broken become masters at mending. Unfortunately, most people won't become who they want because they are too attached to who they've been. Lisa shows you how to let go, how to forgive and how to truly look for the hand of God in your situation, realizing you're never alone. God has a way of making all things work together for your good.

"I did not know the former Lisa who battled such darkness. In fact, it's her joy that sets her apart and her laugh that is contagious. This book is a true testament of how walking in forgiveness can set your life on a whole new trajectory. She truly is what I would call broken, mended and made whole. I highly recommend you read this book as a reminder that you can't undo the past, but you can make the rest of your life the best of your life."

TERRI SAVELLE FOY
TERRI SAVELLE FOY MINISTRIES

"When I was a child, I would often go fishing with my dad. He would throw back some of the fish he caught, but about others he would say, "This is a keeper." When I saw the title of Lisa's book, I knew she was referring to Jesus Christ as her Keeper, and I agree wholeheartedly with that. But a secondary meaning to me is that the title is also about Lisa. She was destined from the very beginning to be an extraordinary Holy Ghost woman of God and definitely a "keeper."

"This book is a litany of ways the devil tries to destroy someone from the inside, but Light overcomes darkness, and God had other plans. Every decision we make has repercussions that we have to live with—for good or for bad. Lisa made a series of good decisions that set her free from Satan's grip. Her first and best decision was to make Jesus Christ the Lord and Savior of her flailing life. That brought an anchor of stability that could not be shaken. Secondly, she decided to not just read or even study the Word of God, but to actually apply it to her life. Somewhere along the way, she received the baptism with the Holy Ghost, which catapulted her into a spiritual realm that few reach. The words from God that she has given me, plus her powerful prayers, have had a substantial influence in my ministry and my life.

"Last but not least, her decision to forgive those that had damaged her life was a key to her spiritual success. I use the word 'decision' advisedly, for we each must decide to forgive, and ask the Holy Spirit to help erase those hurts from our hearts as if they never happened. That is a supernatural feat that can only happen through the joint efforts of the person, plus the Person of the Holy Spirit.

"Lisa's decisions to accept Jesus as her Lord, to walk in the Word, to obey the voice of the Holy Spirit, and to forgive all the perpetrators of her grief have brought her to this point of spiritual excellence in her life. Each one of us can follow that same sequence of decisions and end up giving all glory to 'The Keeper.'"

ELIZABETH R. VAUGHAN, M.D.
PRESIDENT, ELIZABETH VAUGHAN MINISTRIES, INC.

Table of Contents

Dedication

There is absolutely no one, other than the following three, to whom this book could ever be dedicated. They are the reason this book was written and will hopefully become a redemptive tool for countless others who need hope.

The first one is my heavenly Father, God. How does one ever fully comprehend a love like His, which has been, is and always will be since the foundation of this world? Thank you, my Father, for loving me enough to bring me into this world and giving me the courage to convey this story.

The second one is my precious Savior, Jesus Christ. You laid down heaven—I can't even imagine—and came into this dark, sin-ridden and hurting world just for me, but also for every human being. What a profound, sacrificial love that not only has forgiven my sins but has paid the price for complete healing—body, soul, mind and spirit. Then to top it off, you continually make prayer and intercession for me. I'm so glad I have all of eternity to say thank you.

And third, the precious Holy Ghost. Truly you have been my counselor and constant companion throughout this journey—patient with me, yet always nudging me on with your heavenly wisdom, showing me continually that the plans are for a good future and filled with hope. Thank you for your unending out-pouring into my life.

Acknowlegments

———

This book would not have ever been possible without the love and encouragement from the following precious people the Lord has placed in my life. To say that I am grateful beyond words is a massive understatement, but I pray each and every one of them will know from my heart how much I appreciate them and love them to the moon and back.

At the top of this list is my husband Marty. Without his consistent love and gentle encouragement to pursue telling my story, it would have been difficult to even imagine doing this. Thank you, honey. MUAH!

Thank you to Pastors Bob and Joy Nichols of Calvary Cathedral International. Their godly, faithful and loving examples in our lives have nurtured us, encouraged us and taught us God's love never fails, and that nothing is impossible with God. We thank God for your commitment to walking in faith and the love of God for us.

Next are those I call my "Eagle Friends." These are friends who fly at a different altitude with the Lord. They love unconditionally and challenge me to seek His ways, His Word and His love in everything I do, including this book. Without their love, prayers and friendships, the courage to live out my life would have been much harder to find. Thank you from the bottom of my heart for being my friends: Heather Acosta, Debbie Blue, Karol Genovese DelReal, Christy Gaffey, Judy Hall, Jan Johnson, Trish Keiger,

Lindy Manasco, Regina Page, Sandy Pavlick, Laurie Prior, Ruth Simmons, and Dr. Elizabeth Vaughan.

Fourth, but definitely not last, are those I have called "My Book Angels." These precious ones have either encouraged me long term or very specifically with spot-on prophetic words from the Lord about this book. Their encouragement over time has helped fuel me with the courage to move forward and actually do this. And to the ones who have spoken into me, hearing the Father when they didn't even know me or that a book was something being considered, thank you for putting a heavenly seal on my heart to know beyond a shadow of a doubt that this was a life assignment and a God idea: Linda Ash, Lisa Osteen Comes, Terri Savelle Foy, Sherrie Garcia, Vicki Leuther, Roseanna Rizzo, Jessica Shook and Pam White.

Foreword

L isa Manasco is a woman that God has used in a very unique way. Through the experiences of life, she has grown into a strong woman of <u>faith and prayer.</u> In over 55 years as founder and pastor of Calvary Cathedral International, I have never seen any woman fight harder to restore her marriage. I have seen her struggles turn her into a woman of faith, hope and love.

Lisa has steadfastly believed that all things are possible to those who dare to believe God's promises and just don't quit. She is quick to remind every reader that for any difficult situation to work out, you must be born again (John 3:3, 7; Romans 10:9-10) and that forgiveness is a must (Mark 11:25). <u>Nothing works if we are unwilling to forgive.</u>

God has blessed Lisa with a strong marriage, a strong prayer life and a strong ministry. <u>When she prays, Satan trembles!</u> Lisa is an encourager and a minister's friend. I am so blessed to be her pastor.

Read this book and just as Lisa has done, grow stronger in the Lord and the power of His might. This is a must read that will help you grow and become <u>more effective in the end-time harvest.</u>

Lisa is a devoted and caring mother and grandmother and is happily married to her husband, Marty. Joy and I count them as very special faith friends.

—PASTOR BOB NICHOLS, SENIOR PASTOR
CALVARY CATHEDRAL INTERNATIONAL

Introduction

On the pages you are about to turn is my story—my life. I have asked myself and God *numerous* times, "Why in the world should I do this?" After all, I am one in billions of people on this planet, and surely, my story could not be unique or worth telling enough to have to dredge up all these painful memories and events. I have been perfectly content to share one-on-one as the Lord would lead for His glory and healing power, but to put it down in black and white and have it go on into perpetuity is a completely different matter altogether.

Many days, months and even years, I've been wrestling with this, and one answer always comes back to my heart as God patiently keeps saying the word, "Purpose." Every one of us asks in this life, "What is *my* purpose here?" Well for me, telling my life story is at the core of my God-given purpose here on this Earth. It is for such a time as this in *HIStory*, to be told for healing, salvation, deliverance and hope to be restored in those who hear or read it.

Quite honestly, being an "author" is not something I have ever wished for, dreamed about or put on a vision board. Never once in my life have I uttered the words, "I can hardly wait until my book is written and published!" However, what I have slowly come to realize is that sometimes there are gifts and things buried inside us that need to be brought forth and nurtured by God.

Knowing this, God has intermittently stirred this up in me and brought other people as well to encourage me and even speak prophetically into my life—people who don't know me from Adam, much less that this needed to be brought out. Could I have continued my life, ignored this and decided to not write this book? Absolutely! God has given us all free will, and the choice is up to us. However, the Bible says that obedience is better than sacrifice (1 Sam. 15:22).

Really, when it all boils down to the last remaining moment, that one that comes for us all when we take our final breath, will we be able to stand before God and say we have indeed completed our assignments *as He saw them* on Earth? That, my friends, is a regret that can follow us into all of eternity. I for one am not willing to miss hearing His precious words, "Well done, good and faithful servant."

Jesus loved me enough to lay down everything. How then can I not follow His example? If there should be just *one* person who reads this and is set free, then it was worth the pain, the hours and the tears to this point. My prayer is that this book will always find its way to those for whom it was meant, and from these pages, life eternal will spring forth until He returns.

Chapter One

HELP FROM ANOTHER WORLD

W as it knit one and then pearl? I just couldn't seem to remember. I guess, just too much else on my mind. At least Sister's eyes were closed and resting so she couldn't see the tears welling up in my eyes and how bad I really was at knitting!

Funny, how life is a circle—nothing truly random when all is said and done. Life began with my sister's knitting needle intruding into the very source of where my life began...the womb, at the hands of my mother. Mom couldn't bear the thought of having another child, especially not now. With all that had happened in their marriage and lives, better to abort me than to bring a child into such a messed up home, for sure. The knitting needle just happened to be handy, as Sister was always busy at the age of 18, knitting and creating. The plan appeared to be working as Mom began bleeding profusely and went to the hospital, where they sadly announced that at five months into her pregnancy, she was indeed miscarrying, and there was nothing they could do but send her home to finish losing this baby.

Enter God, the sovereign Father of this child—me. Yes, my heavenly Father had a plan way beyond my parents. As a matter of fact, the blueprints originated at the foundation of this Earth. A planned pregnancy by a loving Father, and no one could stop what He had begun and breathed life into. So as Mom awaited the finality of my life, God was protecting and carrying me through, to come out alive from this place called 'the womb.'

Two months after they sent her home to miscarry, I was delivered, albeit very early and barely five pounds, which quickly spiraled down to 3 pounds in an incubator. Now mind you, this was back in 1960, and although there had been some advances, modern NICU care as we now know it was not available.

And so began the journey of my life, in a place where darkness and death searched to eliminate me before I would see the light of day. Ah, but don't feel sorry for me here or tear up in pity because, although this journey has been tumultuous at times, all that I've learned of God's love just for me has become so precious I would not trade one single event of my life, no matter how difficult it may have been. Because of His love for me, the help I've always needed, regardless of the circumstance, has always been there!

The beginning of my life and the failed attempt to eradicate me was kept from me for years—until finally, Sister couldn't contain the false sense of guilt anymore. You see the enemy (the devil) had convinced her that if her knitting needles had not been left out and so accessible to our mother, supposedly, it never would have happened. Ridiculous, isn't it? To think she had any part of or could have ever changed what Mom would do. The truth be known, she would have found a way regardless because the enemy had convinced Mom that she couldn't handle any more in her broken life as well.

So, one night when I was in my early thirties, after Sister had been drinking some, she told me this dark, hidden family secret... that Mom had tried to abort me all those years ago with *her* knitting needles. Shock really doesn't do justice to what I felt in those first hours, days, weeks and then on into months. But as stunned as I was, I comforted my sister in those moments and tried desperately to persuade her it had nothing to do with her at all.

Time froze in that initial unveiling of this secret. I even thought, *Maybe I didn't hear her right.* No. After she repeated the story again, I realized I was hearing right. And I was wide awake. It wasn't a nightmare. Yet it was....

History and all its details flooded my mind as I sat, now years later, watching my sister die of cancer. Decades had passed since that horrible night, but love and forgiveness had always kept our relationship together.

Sister had always wanted me to learn how to knit. She dearly loved this pastime and really was excellent at it, winning blue ribbons at the State Fair. It was all that was left that I could think of to do in her final weeks of life to bring her some joy. So I asked her dear friend Linda to teach me how to knit, then I would be able to sit and knit by her bedside while she struggled to live.

Sister's eyes lit up every time I took the simple mint-green prayer shawl project out of my bag. Peace that really surpassed all natural description blanketed her countenance and her face as she heard my needles clicking together. The irony of it all was that somehow it brought me full circle to a place of peace, knowing that both of us had now seen a turning of events in life that only God can do: What the enemy of our souls meant for destruction was now, in that very moment of sitting by her bedside knitting, bringing peace to Sister and all the glory to God! After all, it says in the Bible, "You made all the delicate, inner parts of my body and knit me together in my mother's womb," (Psalm 139:13 NLT).

The very first time I found that scripture, I was certain that it was absolutely written only for me! The sweet truth is that it's for everyone. The only problem being, there was nothing I could do to save Sister's life the way God had saved mine. We had prayed for healing, but truth be known, she really wanted to go on and be with her husband, our parents and the rest of our family in heaven. The Lord was so gracious in those weeks. He opened her heart and allowed me to lead her to Jesus as her Savior. Hallelujah!

In that moment, came the seal on a prayer that I had believed for God to answer for many, many years—her knowing Jesus as her personal Lord and Savior. Just weeks before she passed, we prayed at her bedside in the hospital. Such peace washed over her soul in those moments, which were heaven-sent for her and for me. Now her eternity was settled and release could come for both of us!

I thank God for His grace to endure in prayer some twenty-plus years for her salvation. Eternity is too important to become weary in prayer for a soul. So, should you be reading this and tempted to stop or wonder if your prayers for your loved ones are working because it's been perhaps even years since you started your prayer journey for them, don't stop! God's Word does not return without accomplishing His intentions, and His timing in their lives will come to pass to secure their future in heaven.

It turns out, I was the firstborn among the Christians in my family tree in a couple of generations, which explains why the enemy of my soul was not so excited about my birthday happening! Satan isn't omniscient or omnipresent, but I believe he can sense when a certain seed has heaven's hand upon it. He desires to keep generations lost and from knowing and serving the Lord. He absolutely hates to lose generational strongholds.

Thank God for praying grandmas! I had one, my mother's mom—a Baptist, Holy Ghost praying farmer's wife, who arose in the early hours of the morning and would sit in a chair, her head bowed, praying with her Bible in her apron-clad lap. With all my heart, I believe it was her prayers for me and this family that went before us to undergird my family and bring us to the feet of Jesus. She has long since gone home to be with the Lord, but her precious Bible lies open on an antique desk of mine from childhood in the entryway of our home. Her faithfulness lives on as she is in the cloud of witnesses in heaven that surrounds and overlooks my family.

Don't you dare give up! Eternity is counting on your prayers to help birth your loved ones into God's kingdom, and He will perform it. When you focus your eyes on Jesus, His help always comes!

Chapter Two

———

THE CREATOR IS ON YOUR SIDE

There are moments in life that mark a soul and can mold a spirit. As I sit here typing, on a God-orchestrated weekend, my view is the amazing Dallas skyline from the 21st floor. Just below is Elm Street and the infamous Dealey Plaza where John F. Kennedy was assassinated. Ironically, in all the years I have lived in Texas, I've always wanted to visit this historical place. As only the Lord can do, I now can say I have had the bird's-eye view of that horrible moment in 1963.

Looking down upon it, what struck me was how quickly I could recount, even though I was only three, where I was the day he was killed. Instantly, I was propelled back 53 years to our living room and coffee table, where my parents bribed me with pretzel rods and candy galore to keep me quiet so they could watch the black and white, nonstop report on the television. Like most Americans that day, time seemed to be in slow motion in what would become one of our nation's darkest moments.

Isn't it astounding how a sight, a smell, a sound can transport you into a vivid memory? Later on in my life and equally as ironic, the Dallas skyline and the premiere of the famous show, Dallas, starring JR would draw me to move to this intriguing place. And many years later, I would actually meet and become friends with Roseanna, the woman who played the housekeeper on that show! She would, in fact, be one of the very first people to encourage me to tell my story and help give me the courage to do it! That is what this book and my story is—a recounting of memories and markings of not only what happened, but how God surrounded me, kept me, healed me and never stopped chasing me with His unconditional love.

Now, lest you think I'm doing this for some kind of kudos, let me assure you, this is strictly for the Lord and His call and assignments on my life—for you!! This is not about yours truly as much as it is about YOU. Your heavenly Father wants you to know beyond a shadow of a doubt that He loves you by the time you finish reading this book. He can heal you and take you through whatever the enemy has thrown your way and *keep* you unto Him for the rest of your life!

Really, it doesn't matter what has sought to destroy you—abuse, rape, alcohol, divorce, drugs, rejection from the womb—He has already paid the price for you to be set free, healed and restored in life. The One who has watched over you since the beginning will not slumber or sleep. You can trust your heavenly Father, even if your earthly one may have failed.

My earthly father was far from perfect and was himself a disappointed and wounded soul. His daddy left him, his sister and their mom at very young ages, forcing him as a young teenager in the 1930s, to become the bread winner for his mom and sister. His

15

mom tried for a short period to help run a family dry cleaning business in North Canton, Ohio. That quickly fell apart, as she literally lost her mind, gave up and ended up in a nursing home for the next 60 years of her life! Yes, I said 60 years in a nursing home from mental issues. Her body was healthy, and she lived to be 98 and outlived both my dad and my Aunt Midge. It was at the age of 97, shortly after I was saved, that I led her to the Lord in the opposite wing of the same nursing home where my own mother was.

Hallelujah!

My earthly daddy died of a heart attack right in front of me just a few months after my 9th birthday. That was my first experience with death, watching him pass as my mother frantically screamed for me to call the ambulance while she tried to revive him with pills on the landing at the top of the stairs. His life was filled with alcohol, promiscuity and broken dreams. I actually have very few memories of him sober, mostly drunk, but he was a nice drunk! (Hey, you take whatever good you can sometimes.)

In the time he spent with me at least he was laughing or playing with me, and for that I'm grateful. I can honestly say I loved my dad what little time I had him in my life. What I've come to see and hopefully learn from watching their lives and my own is that hurt people hurt people, as Joyce Meyer says! Therefore, unless someone in the family tree and cycle chooses to be healed, forgive and follow God's plan, the pain and the cycle of woundedness continues to devour the generations. "Yup," I can almost hear some of you say, "But you don't know what I've done because of all that stuff you're talking about. I've gone too far down the wrong road."

Guess what? You can't go so far that God doesn't still absolutely love you, and He will chase you down. Just stop! Let Him catch you and throw His arms around you. He's not surprised or repulsed by your sin. He's just sad for you because He knows that within a moment's time of you handing it all over to Him and placing yourself in His loving care, all of that can be washed away, and you can be made white as snow (Psalms 51:7).

Ask King David. That's why He wrote that psalm. He had committed adultery and so much more when he wrote it. Then he discovered the power of God's forgiveness and love! That's what God's grace through His only Son, Jesus, was all about—the cross, where it can be as though your sin never happened. There's only one thing you have to do: Receive the gift and never look back because the plans He has for you are for a good future and not for evil (Jer. 29:11).

There's a whole lot that I wish I had never done, just like King David, but I can't undo it. It was pretty ugly for me B.C.— before Christ. When your soul is wounded and your spirit broken, the enemy makes sure you are driven to try and find something to fill the hole in your heart: alcohol, relationships, addictions of any kind. The problem being, none of that can or ever will fix what is broken. But what I was able to do was let Him wash me and forgive me, and forgive myself (That is a biggie!) and move forward, not perfectly mind you by any stretch of the imagination, but forward, knowing that all things really can work together for good for those who are called according to His purpose! (Rom. 8:28)

Listen, God is the biggest fan of recycling in the universe. Who do you think it was, after the fall of man in the Garden of Eden, that came up with the cross and Jesus taking our place so we could once again have an intimate relationship with our heavenly Father? If that's not the best example of recycling, I don't know what is!

God never throws anyone into the trash can. He always chooses to upcycle and recycle lives into something far beyond their wildest imaginations. He is well able to deliver you from the hooks of absolutely any kind of addiction the enemy may have used to try to medicate your pain. He can set you free, and He can *keep* you free. He is The Keeper.

If you stop and really think about it, God keeps us before we even know He's keeping us, or a lot of us would have been dead before we even got the chance to receive Jesus!

Chapter Three

DYSFUNCTION IS
SPELLED SECRETS

F
ear gripped me, standing on the banks of Lake Ontario—
the backyard of our family home—as my brother Stephen
slipped under the water. He was an epileptic and partially,
mentally handicapped due to issues at birth and falling from a top
bunk bed at an early age.

Again though, this was a hidden story nobody in my family
ever wanted to talk about. Dysfunction is really spelled secrets.

Anyhow, there I stood, now age 7, watching him start to
drown as I screamed for Dad to hurry from the shore to save him.
I dearly loved my precious brother, although I never got to see him
or spend much time with him because he didn't live with us by the
time I came along. Sadly, Dad was very ashamed that his only son,
out of four children, was less than perfect and wouldn't be able to
follow in his footsteps or fulfill the dreams he had for him. So it had
been decided that a special school/institution would be best for
him to live in. In my very early years, that was in Leesburg,

Virginia, but later after Dad died, Mom moved him to New York, a couple of hours from where we lived. We would bring him home for holidays and sometimes for long weekends, but less frequently after Dad was gone.

Being the baby in the family, I longed for siblings to be around. My sister Carolyn, the one who loved to knit, was 18 years older than me, and Stephen was twelve years older than me. The firstborn, sister Peggy, would never live past the age of three, due to inverted chicken pox that suffocated her as she slept in her crib.

You can't make this stuff up, people! The devil hated my family and killed and destroyed in some of the most atrocious and bizarre ways. I'm sure Hollywood would pay big bucks for a script with so many wild twists and turns!

Even though Dad was able to rescue Stephen in time from the grand mal seizure that pulled him under the lake, this incident opened one of the first doors to fear in my life. Although, I'm sure the original entrance for the spirit of fear was in the womb for me, this event with my brother began to magnify the size of the fear in my life.

It became clear to me at a very young age that you never know how or when tragedy will strike. Carefree play for me was guarded, and expectations were always kept low in my world. For me, survival was the key focus, not what toy, new place or vacation might be in my future, or how much my parents loved me. Disappointment, at best, was sure to come. And in my childhood mind, that was really the best I could hope for, let alone some bigger life events—death, abuse, etc.

Fear paralyzed me, as I would later understand as an adult, and kept me from anything like the luxury of dreaming or feeling safe. There was no thriving, simply the art of surviving. The whispers of fear were continual throughout my growing up, which would launch me early headlong into anything that could numb me or make me forget the craziness at home. Our home was clearly not a genuine, Christian home in any respect. Religious yes, but not loving or Christian in actuality. We belonged to the Catholic Church in a small town in upstate New York, and there wasn't any harbor of solace or help there as it would turn out either.

Instead, it furthered the presence of fear. Let me say very plainly here: I'm not bashing the Catholic Church, as I know there are some wonderful, born-again and spirit-filled Catholic churches. This is my personal story of what I was a part of growing up. The priest I knew was a mean, grouchy old man, and on one very special occasion, scared the living daylights out of me! The occasion was a first communion class at about age eight.

To take part in this important ceremony, several instructional classes were required. This particular day, it was all about the Trinity. As Father Foley approached the chalk board in front of the pews in this little white church, he abruptly picked up a big, fat piece of chalk, and said, "Today you're going to learn about the Father, the Son and the Holy Ghost." Then he angrily drew a triangle, pressing so hard with the chalk that it broke!

Wow. I could hardly wait to hear about this spooky, angry trio he just barked about! I really was terrified, sitting there—a little girl wondering what weird and mean things I was going to hear about next. Just what I didn't need in my little world, anything or anybody that even hinted at being strange!

That was my first introduction to the Trinity, which, as the devil made sure for many years to come, would motivate me to move as far away as possible from anything remotely to do with church, God, Jesus and the Holy Ghost! Let me insert here, this is the perfect example of how just one person's representation of God can literally turn somebody in the opposite direction. I pray I never forget this because it speaks to the power of one, me or you, to positively or negatively affect people for our heavenly Father, Jesus and the precious Holy Spirit.

I can actually laugh looking back on it now, but mind you, it really terrified me at the time and further convinced me, via the devil's whispers, that there was no love, no hope and certainly not a God that would want me or that I would want.

It's so vital that each one of us remembers that we might actually be the only picture of Jesus that someone will see. So we need to be mindful we show them something that will draw them to Him. Unconditional love, grace, a dose of His mercy, given in just a moment's time, can be the very hope and chance of future change they could have.

What might have happened differently if Father Foley had been gentle, kind and loving that day he taught on the Trinity? It might have just given this little girl a real glimmer of the love my heavenly Father has for me at a much earlier age. Do I blame him entirely? Of course not. I'm simply saying we underestimate the power of showing God's love every time we have the opportunity.

Reflecting on Father Foley, I wonder where someone in his life missed the chance to show him the real love of the Father. There's always a domino effect, whether we choose to believe it or not. Really, how much must our Father God, Jesus and the Holy Spirit be grieved when they watch us do or say anything other than the absolute source of love they are?

"For none of us lives to himself, and not one dies to himself," (Rom. 14:7). We are not islands; we are all a part and absolutely instrumental in a universal story that is constantly unfolding. What part will you play today for that lady behind the counter at the bank or grocery store? Will you reveal love, hope and grace, or will you be remote, anxious and in a hurry to get about your list of errands?

It's entirely our choice, moment by moment and day by day, if we will show people a glimpse of His love and hope.

Chapter Four

THE VALLEY OF THE
SHADOW OF DEATH

A lthough there were a lot of negative events and memories of my mother, there is one good one that I love to pull from the archives of my heart. Very often on Sunday afternoons, she would pop popcorn in a pan over the stove, smother it promptly with melted butter and oodles of salt, and then play a game of Scrabble on the living room coffee table with me. It's the only interactive memory I have of Mom actually spending time doing something with me while growing up.

There we would sit, me on the rug and her on the couch, eating popcorn from an old wooden bowl, playing Scrabble. I love this picture, and I share it because it is vital that you ask the Lord to help you find even one good, pleasurable memory with your family if you've been through a lot of negative and painful experiences in your childhood. The reason being, the enemy always magnifies all the negative, usually to the point that being able to heal or honor your parents can become difficult or seemingly impossible.

The truth is there is always something good to recall, even if it's as simple as them reading a book, buying you a new pair of shoes, or making sure you were always fed. <u>Parents parent the best they can at the time with whatever source of reference they had growing up.</u>

Boy, let me tell you, that became an even greater revelation as I began to parent my two boys. No matter how much you may love them, it can be challenging to teach and show them all that's in your heart for them, especially if you never had it.

Mom grew up on a farm in Hillsdale, Michigan, with two younger brothers. She met my dad after she had completed business school, and fell deeply in love with this skinny, dashing, outgoing inventor. The love she had in those early days was so great that we, years later, found poetry about her love and then sonnets from the beginning of her disappointed and broken heart. These surfaced in a family trunk, tucked away in Sister's basement, and oddly enough became a tool that the Lord used to show me her broken heart and life. Remember, hurt people hurt people!

The loss of their first child, my sister Peggy, became the first of several events causing Mom to become permanently broken. It broke her in such a way that everything that followed in their marriage and lives eroded her into the shell of a woman I saw by the time I came along.

Grandma Moore, my dad's mom, who was a smashed mess herself, chose to blame Mom for my sister Peggy's death. The demonic guilt and pounding that followed for Mom, I'm sure was heart wrenching. Again let me point out the domino effect—had Grandma been able to rise up and know the Lord's healing in her own life, she might have been able to console my mom and dad instead of condemning them at such a pivotal point in their lives.

Not only that, but Grandma horribly reaped what she sowed in judging Mom for Peggy's death. Her two children both passed away in an untimely fashion, and she outlived them both. It is an absolute truth, "judge not lest you be judged in the same manner!" (Matt. 7:1)

In those days, Mom began to lose herself, her interests, her passions and her personal giftings. That is the most dangerous place you can go. God puts certain passions, interests and giftings in each one of us. They tend to be things we like to do and that invigorate us. God put them there, ultimately, to use for His purpose and glory. So when we become so wounded in life that we stop even enjoying those things, we go into limbo. We shift the gear to neutral and only survive, not thrive or become what the Lord intended us to be. How do I know this? Because I not only watched Grandma and my mom do this, I entered that zone for several years myself.

Disappointment in my adult years would continue in different ways, and isolating myself, nesting on a red couch would become my safety. There's nothing wrong with red couches, mind you; I still have two of them. It's just that now, Mama doesn't sit on it to hide! Funny how powerful a picture can be in a person's life because growing up, my mom did the very same thing. She would sit on an ugly grey couch, but she would also smoke three packs of cigarettes a day!

Thank God, I at least skipped the smoking. Vanity helped me there in the sense that the smell was so gross on and around Mom, I vowed I wasn't going to ever do that! So... I picked a prettier couch and no cigarettes. Same outcome though, it just didn't smell quite as bad!

"How can you joke about things like that," you might ask? Let me tell you, laughter can literally be a lifesaver when craziness constantly encroaches on your life. The Bible says that laughter (a cheerful heart) does good like a medicine (Prov. 17:22), and medical science has even backed the Lord up on that. So go ahead and be sure you laugh, chuckle and find the humor, even in the ugly times. It is a medicine that God can use to keep you from quitting, going crazy or not caring anymore!

Layers of traumatic times would continue to put my mom in a downward spiral. My brother's physical handicaps furthered her sense of guilt because there would be no perfect son for my dad. The distance in their marriage became so vast that although Dad was seeing success in his professional life as an inventor, he sought and found a relationship outside their marriage that ironically produced another son. Mom became fully aware and painfully damaged when this devastating truth was revealed at my dad's death.

The first indication was a picture found in his desk. Then, as I was later told, this other woman and the young boy turned up at the visitation at the funeral home. Seriously, even now as I recount this, I think this is literally like a movie drama being played out. Can you imagine? I can unfortunately. Yet it gave me a compassion that would later help me forgive my mom for how she had wounded me, and then lead her to the Lord. All things really can work together for good, if you let them, and you let Him.

The following years, growing up with just mom and me, were painfully lonely and her emotions were no longer viable to the outside world. I can't ever recall her actually telling me she loved me. The first year after Dad died was particularly difficult for me.

I was in third grade at the time and soon learned that I had an undeveloped part of my eye, diagnosed from birth, which would require bifocal glasses. They didn't give any hope that this would ever change and said that glasses would become a standard for my life. This was not good news for a nine-year-old, bashful girl who had just lost her daddy. I felt certain those glasses would ensure nobody would ever want to be my friend. The ugly duckling seemed to be taking on an ugly life all its own!

I had no sooner become subject to this new outlook, when within the same month our neighbor down the road had gotten drunk, and she hit and killed my dog! Can you say bad country and western song gone amuck? That was all at age nine—Dad died, bifocal glasses and my beloved Brandy killed by a drunk neighbor.

Don't tell me God isn't a keeping God. I know He is because I sit here, serving Him, healed by Him, and knowing His eternal love for me! I'm not saying I'm perfect or that I've arrived. What I'm saying is: Life is a journey, and as long as you set your heart toward God and keep moving, victories come. The truth is, there are much, much worse life stories in the world than mine, and yet there is not one person out there that God can't heal, deliver and turn around!

As bleak as that year seemed to a nine-year-old little girl, God intervened and gave me an amazing best friend! Enter Nancy, who would become my BFF in the third grade. She became one of my happy memories and a friendship that would have hours and hours of fun and silly laughter. What a gift to me in a life that had known no laughter or true joy to that point.

God knows just what we need and when we need it to help us keep moving forward in life. Recently, I returned for my 40-year high school reunion and caught up with this dear friend and her husband. Some of the same wonderful laughter ensued and usually over silly things again! During this timely visit, she began to reminisce about when my dad passed away, and as she did, another friend at the table said, "Nancy, you should tell her about your memory of her dad's shoes."

Naturally, this peeked my interest as I had never heard her mention this. She began to share how two weeks after my dad had passed away, she had come over to our house for a sleepover, and when she came through the door, she noticed that my dad's shoes were still sitting near the front door—two weeks after he had died. She shared how strange she thought it was that my mother didn't put them somewhere out of sight by then. Having pondered this and wondered myself why that would have been, it began to show what a paralyzing event it was for my mother. So much so that she didn't think to remove the shoes from our daily path, and instead left them there, perhaps in some kind of hope he would return and put them on again.

This story, though seemingly insignificant, helped me yet again see into my mother's frame of mind and spirit at that time. No doubt, his passing introduced a new level of depression and hopelessness that my mother would never recover from in her lifetime.

Life moved on, and I graduated from high school and moved to Buffalo, graduating from a business school after two years. After I moved out from living with Mom, she had multiple, ongoing strokes to the point that Sister and I had to move her into a nursing home. She became a vegetable—no speech, couldn't feed herself, and due to paralysis, they had to amputate one of her legs because of gangrene.

By this time, I had moved to Texas with my soon-to-be first husband and had my first son. Throughout all of this, I was desperately searching for love and a normal life. My first marriage dissolved only a year and a half later, leaving me a single mom to my sweet toddler. But in the midst of the pregnancy with my first son, I met someone who would introduce me to Jesus and begin to forever change the course of my life!

Enter Karol. She and her husband were living in the apartment under us, and she and I met at the pool one hot, Texas day. I was very, very pregnant! Karol struck up a conversation, and before long, she was sharing how Jesus had made a difference in their lives, and she wanted me to know He could change mine too. Honestly, I was pretty leery and standoffish at first and just tried to remain polite. Within the next few weeks, we would find ourselves at a large church in Fort Worth, called Calvary Cathedral International, pastored by Pastor Bob and Joy Nichols.

Karol had led me to the Lord, and I had prayed the prayer of salvation and for a short few weeks was beginning to walk with Him. That waned, however, and because my marriage was in jeopardy, I laid down any further journey with the Lord. Later on, the Lord restored me and my second husband back to this church with the faith-filled pastors teaching us, praying for us and loving us in our journey with the Lord! God truly does restore all things, but now back to the story at hand.

Those days were raw and empty as divorce was imminent, and there was no family to support me in this scary place. Sister was busy trying to find some love and normalcy for her own life in Valdosta, Georgia, during this time, and of course Mom no longer even knew I existed because of her condition. Desperate and empty really don't fully describe where I was at that time, but even then,

God was chasing me, keeping me and watching over me and my son. Somehow by the grace of God, I managed to get a job at a local bank and room with a girlfriend from work.

It was at this juncture, I met my current husband of almost 32 years. More on that season later. What needs to be shared in the retelling of Mom's life and mine is this: As I remarried and really handed my life over and committed it to God, I would soon go back to New York with the sole mission of somehow leading my mother and grandmother to the Lord. Becoming radically saved and discovering His love for me lit my soul on fire for them to somehow come to know Him as their personal Savior. How that could ever happen for either one of them in the condition they were in was seemingly impossible.

But Jesus had become so real, as did eternity and the choice of heaven or hell, that I knew, somehow, I at least had to try. Regardless of the fact that Mom had tried to abort me, and there was never any real emotional normal parental connection, I understood finally now, how she came to the place where she did those things. And I sure didn't want my mama to miss heaven! This was a journey of faith for sure in more ways than one, due to a lack of finances. How could I even travel back to New York from Texas?

But God. Long story short, He supplied a ride back with friends from church who had family themselves not far from where I needed to go. God always makes a way where there appears to be no way. Make no mistake; He will move all of heaven and earth just for one soul!

One very long car ride later, I entered the nursing home where my mom and grandma now both resided. If either of them had known that they were both in the same nursing home, one hallway apart, they would have had an ever-living hissy fit! A mutual hatred for each other had long been in effect because of all I previously shared.

As I walked nervously toward my mother's room first, I began to think maybe I was delusional to think either one of them could ever really be saved. "After all," the devil chided, "one is a vegetable, and one is ancient and crazy!" He had a point. The problem being, that was only a partial truth—what I saw in the natural. It didn't factor in the absolute truth that God is the "super" to the "natural!" So, I slowly entered Mom's room, desperately trying to remember all the instructions I felt the Lord had given me for this important moment, which wasn't a lot and seemed kind of crazy to me, truth be told. Without faith, it's impossible to please God (Heb. 11:6), and faith steps will definitely smack of some craziness to your natural thinking sometimes!

There she was, sitting up, strapped in a chair by her bed. The strokes had removed any familiar resemblance of what my mom looked like growing up. Her face was distorted, teeth gone, gray and disheveled hair covered her little head, hanging down. No longer dressed in her own clothes but a hospital gown that quickly revealed a stub for her right leg. My heart was flooded instantly with such godly compassion for her. A partial body remained, the mind and speech completely gone for years now. How in the world was I ever going to be able to lead her to the Lord? I would only have three days with her before I had to return home. This looked like it could take three years...if ever.

"Hi, Mom." Nothing. At that moment, I realized yet again she wasn't there for me, but she never had been. This wasn't about me; it was entirely about eternity. I set the flowers down on her bedside table and then sat down on the bed next to her and took her hand. Still no sense that she knew who I was or that she could even understand me. Small talk awkwardly rambled from my lips, as I wondered what the sap I was trying to do!

Suddenly, the Lord gently said to me, "Talk to her from your heart, and ask her to forgive you for being a difficult teenager."

Now mind you, my initial inside reply to Him was, "Ask *her* to forgive *me*? Really? I wasn't all that much of a challenge, and need I remind you, she tried to abort *me*?" Thank God for His grace! He said, "Look at her, and tell me you can't do this." Ouch. Tears filled my eyes as I asked the Lord to forgive me—and of course, He did.

"Mama," I began. "I need to ask you to forgive me for being so difficult as a teenager. Will you please forgive me?"

She lifted her head at this point and glanced at me with an empty stare. No words came from her as she continued to seem far removed. I quietly sat there for several minutes, saying nothing, just holding her hand. Then it was my turn to speak forgiveness to her from me. "Mom, I want you to know I forgive you for trying to abort me."

Then the Lord said, "Now go ahead and share Jesus with her, the same way you would with a five-year-old."

I leaned forward and with every heart string engaged, I said, "Mama, you know Jesus is real, and He loves you. He died for you and has forgiven you. I have asked Him into my heart. Would you like to ask Him into your heart?"

As God and heaven was my witness, she lifted her head toward me and said the only word she would speak in three days, "Yes."

To this day, that is the sweetest 'yes' I've ever heard. I then prayed the prayer of salvation with her and sealed her for heaven. Tears poured from my eyes with gratitude to the Lord for this miraculous moment.

Still sitting on the side of the bed, I tried to compose myself, when suddenly the devil said, "What makes you think that was real? Look at her!"

I instantly knew the answer by God's grace, and said back to him, "Well, it must have been real or you wouldn't have shown up to challenge it. It is done!"

From that moment forward, never have I ever doubted that she went home to be with the Lord when she passed away. The Keeper had kept my mama through all those tumultuous years until she could receive Jesus. She now awaits her baby girl in the cloud of witnesses. (Mom, it'll be a while. Gotta finish my assignment first.)

The next time I see her, she'll be young, with beautiful red hair, a whole body, a healed heart and a smile that fills half of heaven! Think I'll go pop some popcorn now, and toss it into that old wooden bowl the Lord managed to salvage just for me, and thank God for all He has done!

Chapter Five

HIS TIMING
SHELTERS YOUR LIFE

I stopped at the nurse's station and asked which room my grandmother was in. They politely directed me down an adjacent hallway from my mother's room. Ten years at least had passed since I had seen Grandma. Memories of visiting her growing up suddenly surfaced from all those years before. Her home was a nursing home for 60 years of her 98-year-long life. She simply had mentally checked out due to all the rejection and pain in her life.

Back in the very early days, I was told they tried to give her those old fashioned shock treatments to try and pull her out, but to no avail. Prior to my arrival into this family, they used to try and bring her home to our house from the nursing home on Sundays.

One particular Sunday, as the story from the dysfunctional family skeleton closet goes, they had picked her up that morning to hopefully take her with them to Mass. She was having no part of that, so my parents left her behind at the house while they went ahead to church. Never ever, not ever, should you leave a crazy, broken grandmother home alone! Disaster is sure to follow, and it did. While my parents were at Mass for that short hour, what could possibly happen? Apparently, Grandma was emotionally flooded from hell itself with a need to express, yet again, how much she disliked my mother and all that she was and did. So what does an angry, demented mother-in-law do? She decided to show her contempt for my mother's decorating taste in the kitchen curtains. Had she simply torn them down, that would have made a point, but shoot, hell didn't think that was dramatic enough—so she set them on fire! She apparently realized, as the flames engulfed the entire kitchen, she was in danger of the whole house burning down, so she quickly got lucid enough to call the fire department!

As my parents pulled in from church, they found Grandma in the yard and the firemen blasting the kitchen with water. When dad asked her what in the world happened, she said, "I didn't like Norma's curtains, so I set them on fire." Nice. I'm sure the commandment, 'thou shall not kill,' suddenly became an option my mother in particular would have been willing to attempt and say her rosary later!

Fast forward decades later, they cohabited the same nursing home. Ironic how the very things and people we sometimes try so hard to ignore, not forgive or reason away return to haunt us. Forgiveness is really not optional; it is absolutely necessary in being able to move forward with any kind of peace or blessing in our lives. And this was a textbook example of how badly and how sadly it can and will turn out when forgiveness isn't chosen.

Charred curtains, accusations and all, we are commanded to forgive as an act of our will. It's those nasty emotions that seek to eat our lunch and keep us captive! "Be kind and compassionate to one another, forgiving each other, just as in Christ God forgave you," (Eph. 4:32 NIV).

I had absolutely no expectations that she would remember me at all as I walked down the hallway to Grandma's room. This visit would be as though I was visiting a stranger, simply out of respect and the love God put in my heart that her soul needed to know Jesus. What a complete waste to live that long and then go on into eternity in hell. At the very least, if she accepted Jesus that day, she could go on to heaven and be relieved of all the misery she had known in this life.

As I entered her room, I saw her in the bed right by the door, curled up in a fetal position. The nurse by her bedside asked who I was looking for, and she quickly confirmed this was Conradine, better known as my grandma. The surprise was evident on the nurse's face, as she couldn't believe anyone had come to visit her— such a sad statement in itself.

The nurse said, "Let me see if I can rouse her," and started calling out her name, leaning over the rail, explaining her grand-daughter was here to visit. She told her my name, and to my utter shock Grandma said, "Wendell's daughter?"

"Yes," I said. "Grandma, its Lisa, Wendell's youngest daughter." She started to try and lift herself in the bed and look at me, and my heart melted for this tiny, wrinkled, little old lady looking up at me. She was genuinely happy to see me and a glimmer tried to peek through cloudy, cataract-ridden eyes. The sweet nurse interjected and offered to get her out of the bed and into a wheelchair. The thought of that looked pretty precarious to me at best, as she seemed so frail. But the nurse said she was able, and that at times, they still tried to wheel her down to the community room so she could get a change of scenery.

"Tell you what," the nurse said. "She loves to drink hot tea. How about we take her down to the community sunroom, I'll bring you both some tea and you can visit your grandma?"

Finally, what was about to transpire in this short visit with my grandmother would almost seem like a normal and sweet memory to have of her. It would be our very last time together.

The sunroom was indeed sunny that day and miraculously empty of anybody else as we got situated across from each other to visit over our tea. She was clear as a bell and seemed grateful to have a visitor—a miracle in itself. I began to share with her about my life, that I was married and had an adorable little boy, who was her great-grandson.

She listened and nodded and responded with kindness. Sadly, conversation ran out quickly, as past the informational pieces of news, there just was nothing much left to say. I was okay with that though, as we quietly sat sipping tea on that sunny day. Just being able to have this little window of time with her in a lucid moment was, in fact, a gift from God to me and, I believe, to her as well.

In the midst of enjoying our tea, the Lord nudged me that it was time to share Jesus with her in the same simple way I had with Mom just shortly before.

"Grandma, I want to share with you something awesome that has happened to me. Not long ago, I discovered that Jesus is as real as you and me sitting right here and that He's forgiven me for all my sin. He has loved me more than anyone could, and I've asked Him into my heart as my Savior. Would you like to ask Him into your heart today and be forgiven?"

She looked me straight in the face, and said, "I would really like that, yes."

Sitting in a sunny room over a cup of tea, I led my grandma, at the age of 96, in the prayer of salvation! Jesus and I were two for two that day, and I was sure heaven must be rejoicing over my family. What a day! Suddenly, hell was depopulated of my precious family members, and heaven gained new daughters. We finished our tea, and I wheeled her back to her room and hugged her goodbye for the last time on this side of heaven.

In an instant, all the craziness that had gone on between us in all those years could now be redeemed—all because Jesus chose to go to that cross and bear it all for us to be set free, healed and delivered from the enemy.

It didn't mean that their still weren't memories and issues for me to overcome in the days ahead, but what it so clearly did define for me is that God can and will do anything for us because He loves us with an everlasting and eternal love. Each and every human being, no matter how abused, broken or torn, is able to be made whole and redeemed!

MOM AND DAD (WEDDING PICTURE).

MOM AND ME (AGE 3) IN 1963 AT MY BROTHER,
STEPHEN'S SCHOOL IN LEESBURG, VIRGINIA.

MY FIRST COMMUNION, MAY 26, 1968, WITH MY SISTER CAROLYN.

ME AT AGE 8 WITH BY BELOVED DOG, BRANDY, FEBRUARY 1968.

FOUR GENERATIONS – MY GRANDMA WATKINS,
MOM, MY NIECE BONNIE AND ME.

MY BROTHER STEPHEN AND ME IN THE MID-1960S.

DAD (WENDELL MOORE) AND HIS INVENTION - THE ROCKET BELT.

DAD TEST FLYING THE ROCKET BELT.

MY GRANDMA MOORE (ON THE LEFT),
GREAT UNCLE LES AND ANOTHER RELATIVE – OCTOBER 1967.

MOM AND DAD – OCTOBER 1967.

ME AND MY BROTHER STEPHEN.

ME AND MY SISTER CAROLYN.

ME, MY SON ROBERT (AGE 15), MY SON JOHN (AGE 5)
AND MY SISTER CAROLYN AT THE BUFFALO SCIENCE MUSEUM,
JULY 4TH WEEKEND 1998.

Chapter Six

HE NEVER SLEEPS

T he reason it is important that I tell my story, again, is not to gain sympathy or pity, nor is it to portray myself as a victim. In fact, if that's what you are seeing or feeling, set this book down and move on. The reason it's important is to show you that I'm the victor out of all this.

These layers of stories are to bring hope to the hopeless and the revelation that God can take anybody out of anything and turn it completely around in your own heart—ultimately for His glory. The truth be known, I'm actually a pretty private person, and I share precious little with precious few. The Lord had to do some serious nudging and speaking for this book to be written. But when He wakes you up at 3 a.m. and gives you the title and scripture for a book, it's time to get serious and pay attention to the assignment at hand!

The astounding thing to me, as I go back and recount all this, is that in some ways it doesn't even feel like it's me or my life. It's as though I'm watching and retelling the story from the audience as it plays out on the stage of my spirit to share! That's how deeply God can heal and set you free—as though you are observing someone else's life long ago.

Fear is the basis of all that the enemy ever seeks to establish in our lives. In fact, it's the foundation he is always trying to reinforce. If he can inspire enough rejection, abuse or pain in your life, it can and will lock you away from the love of God and His plans for you. But perfect love casts out fear because fear brings torment (1 Jn. 4:18), and I can surely attest to that! Torment ensues. The earlier in a person's life the foundation and layers of fear are laid, the more it can affect your adult life. *But God...!*

One of the perspectives the enemy loves to destroy with fear is the image we have of our earthly fathers. He uses this because he knows that it carries over into how we perceive our heavenly Father. If he can establish rejection, lack of trust and abandonment through an earthly father, he has an excellent chance of destroying our belief that our heavenly Father could ever be any different.

That's why it was no surprise, looking back, how certain events with my dad greatly affected my concept of God. Because he was in my life for only nine short years, that feeling of safety, trusting he would be there for me and really knowing a true father's love, is extremely hard to recall.

He was an inventor, and Dad was definitely a dreamer and a very smart man. After all, you have to be able to think outside the box to create something like the Rocket Belt! My dad is known as the inventor of the jet pack that can be strapped to your back, and make you fly like James Bond so cleverly did in the movie, "Thunderball."

In his short life, Dad went on to meet President John F. Kennedy, Sean Connery and was scheduled to actually meet Walt Disney, I was told. But he passed away just two weeks prior to that appointment. One can only imagine what Mr. Disney had in mind for that meeting!

For Dad, flying was as important as the air he breathed, and he was always envisioning different ways to get a bird's perspective. So growing up with planes around was something quite normal for me—until he passed. He had his own small, private plane, lovingly named Charlie, and there was a plane in our garage as well that he was building and working on in his spare time.

I remember that little red plane called Charlie very well. I would fly with Mom and Dad in it several times those first nine years. We would go to family reunions on my dad's side in Canton, Ohio, from upstate New York. One particular trip though would stand out above the others.

As was often the case when I was around Mom and Dad together, they would end up in a fight. They rarely enjoyed each other's company, and laughter between them was equally as rare. Unfortunately, alcohol was one of the central causes for their arguments to flare. This day was no different. We loaded the car for the drive to the little, local airport, preparing to leave for a family reunion weekend in Canton.

Although it was a bright, sunny summer day, it was a dark and stormy car ride to the airport. Dad was driving drunk, and Mom was yelling that there was no way we were going to get in that plane with him in that condition. *Yeah, right Mom*, I later thought. But for whatever reasons, she relented and strapped me in the back seat of the plane and then crawled in the front next to dad as he started Charlie up.

Why in the world a mother would ever subject herself and her 6-year-old daughter to a certain chance of death, I will never know! A part of me has always thought she had hoped death would come to us that day, and in her thinking, put us all out of the miserable life we knew.

I can still clearly recall my fear in the back seat of the plane. While they continued to fight, we taxied. The fear itself was all-consuming to a six-year-old little girl. Then as we took off down the runway, only minutes into that flight of fear, I instantly went to sleep. It was a touch from my heavenly Father that I know, beyond a shadow of a doubt, He did to protect His little girl from that nightmare.

During the flight to Canton, I never awakened until we were approaching the landing and I saw the lights on the runway. Somehow (God, of course), we landed safely and went on to the family reunion. The Keeper may have put me into a supernatural sleep on that little plane, but He who kept me did not slumber or sleep!

In my adult years, the Lord continually showed me how much He can be trusted as the best Father I could ever hope for. Don't misconstrue this and think I don't honor my earthly father. He was a hurt soul, who ultimately couldn't do any more than he did.

The movie, "Saving Mr. Banks," released in 2013, was a story that opened a flood gate of tears to help heal yet another layer, as I watched it on the big screen. In this true story, based on the author of Mary Poppins, P.L. Travers, Walt Disney relentlessly pursues her to release the rights for him to make the original movie. Travers, as it turned out, had partially based the story on her own father, trying to salvage her dad's image from one of a drunk and neglectful father.

Disney loved the whimsical story of Mary Poppins and would woo her to let him make it into a movie. But as the story unfolds and her memories surface of the truth about her dad, she desperately sought to save her father's image, Mr. Banks.

I cried an ugly, messy cry in the theatre that day. I got it. Except my story would've been called "Saving Mr. Moore," aka: my father.

I tell the details of his life never to dishonor him—I actually believe he would be proud that better choices are now being made in our family. I tell the stories to show the power of God's love to heal. Ironic, isn't it? My heavenly Father wrote the original story. It's called "Saving Lisa!"

Chapter Seven

RESTORING IMPOSSIBLE
BROKEN PLACES

O nce you begin to realize that indeed life is a journey and not a destination, it helps you start moving toward any healing you may need, and also toward the reason the Lord put you on this Earth! There are people, places and callings that are just waiting for you.

It's not all about you, and yet it is! Each one of us is a piece to a puzzle, and all you have to do to understand that is recognize the giftings He's placed in us and grasp how just one person can affect one or many—the Reverend Billy Graham, Thomas Edison, Rosa Parks, just to name a few. They were individuals who stepped out and did what God had put in their hearts to do and became what God wanted them to be. Thank God, they stepped out, or the world as we know it would be very different.

As we move forward into the places the Lord directs, the power of what lies ahead of us is always life and world changing. He desires to reach as many as He possibly can with His unconditional love and delivering power. But He's counting on people like you and me to step out and into the plan He's had for us since the foundation of the Earth.

If you're looking for the perfect moment when all is seemingly settled, you will be waiting a very long time. That perfect place and season doesn't exist—except in your mind. The 28 years I've been walking with the Lord have had great highs and deep valleys. The enemy doesn't leave you alone by any stretch of the imagination, especially if you are running full throttle for the Lord.

Throughout the majority of my walk, one of the biggest goals for me was to be a loving and devoted wife and mom. I've seen so much that I didn't want to repeat in these vital roles, and yet I've missed the mark dreadfully as both my husband and two amazing sons would tell you. Now like most women, that alone could very easily put me back on that red couch until I go home to be with the Lord if I let it. I have asked their forgiveness as it was needed, knowing that if we could at least recognize the things that needed to be corrected, that was a huge leap from where I was growing up.

Being a wife or mother when you have no frame of reference can be challenging at times. Raising two boys and trying to be the parent I never had, while allowing the Father to continue to heal me, was a tricky path. But the one thing my sons can truly say is, even with all the faults I've demonstrated, I love them to the moon and back. And I tell them so! Hopefully, they have learned from the negative as much as the positive examples how to parent their own children. See, our mistakes as parents are where the enemy likes to totally condemn us by continually replaying what we've done wrong.

The Lord gave me a very freeing revelation about this one day—as I trotted around that mountain one more time. He said, "Nothing is lost, even in the negative, if you choose to use it for a teaching tool with them as well." Of course, we all would much rather teach our kids by good and positive examples. But it's so freeing to know that even when we blow it, it's still redeemable!

"There is therefore now no condemnation to them which are in Christ Jesus, who walk not after the flesh, but after the Spirit," (Rom. 8:1 KJV). This is where this scripture came to life for me at another level! Let me tell you, it is the enemy who throws all the mess back up in your face. But I have been washed white as snow (Isa. 1:18), and the Lord has cast my sin as far as the east is from the west (Ps. 103:12), and He remembers it no more! (Heb. 8:12) Somebody say, "Hallelujah!"

If I've only made 50% progress since my parents raised me in all that mess, then praise God, I am 50% farther down the road to complete healing in my family. With me being a praying Mom/Mimi, how can I expect anything but complete victory for my children and grandchildren? When I pray the Word of God over them, it will not return without accomplishing what God intends, and I can expect to see them living for and serving the Lord. I can expect to see them blessed, whole and walking in victory, declaring what the Lord has done!

The same is true in my role as a spouse. If you are reading this and have failed at being a good, godly spouse, let me encourage you there as well. My first marriage failed rather quickly. I was not even close to being in a place to love someone with God's kind of love. There was way too much in me that needed healing before I could give or receive a healthy kind of love in any relationship. That's not to say I didn't want to; I didn't know how to.

That was some 30 years ago, and there is no unforgiveness present for either one of us. That in itself is rarely heard of in this world. God's grace and the love we have for our son was far greater than any complaint or hurt either of us may have had. Our son has been and continues to be a great source of joy.

Right here let me say, if you find yourself divorced, don't add to the pain of the divorce by hanging onto unforgiveness and letting your children see it. I understand that there can be painful feelings and issues. We really had to work at it during our first year. The key was that we worked past any issues, and we let our love for our son and what was best for him rule. God is able to make all grace abound to you for any season and reason. And to this day, my husband and I are friends with my son's father and his wife and are all enjoying this season of parenting and grand-parenting together.

Don't think my marriage of almost 32 years has been a Cinderella story or that I've mastered married life and been waltzing around with a prince in some amazing glass slippers. Not so! However, he is very handsome, and we've had some precious moments in our marriage. But we've also been to the point where it was falling apart—with absolutely no hope of staying together, and weeks away from what seemed to be an imminent divorce.

Although that was years ago, that horrible year comes to the forefront in memories that caused as much pain as my childhood. We both knew the Lord early on in those 32 years. Both of us had been serving Him and attending church for years when things began to unravel into something designed by hell to take us both out. Again, the plot is to displace you from where God, by His grace, has placed you.

Remember, the devil roams about seeking whom he may devour (1 Pet. 5:8), and he will take a mile if you give that snake an inch. Never let your guard down in life. The war in our minds against believing the devil's lies is something that's just a fact on this side of heaven. So you simply must learn to fight the good fight by putting your faith in God and what He says about you. It's no cake walk, but it is all worth it!

The year this all happened, I dubbed early on "my Job year." In the Bible, Job experienced a year of great loss in every area of his life, and found himself even questioning where God was during a time where it seemed as though God had disappeared. Then as he journeyed through the devastation and questioned God, he began to see Him as never before. The love and sovereignty of his God expanded to a depth Job had never before experienced in his heart.

My husband and I made several mistakes and fear-based decisions as a couple that year. After my husband lost his long-time job at the railroad, we made a very unwise and un-counseled decision to move across the country to what we thought the Lord had for him in particular. This was the beginning of absolute hell and hell-sent attacks on our lives. Mind you, when you live your life with total faith in God, you walk in His promises. One of those promises is protection. But we had let our hedge of protection down through fear and then strife. Not a good combo. As we maneuvered through that season, numbing would be the best it would get before the onset of "my Job Year."

Long story short, divorce had been filed for, and then shock began to set in. At the same time, my sweet sister Carolyn called to tell me she had been diagnosed with liver and bone cancer and was not given long to live. As if that weren't enough to test every cell of faith in my body and spirit, my oldest son was going through an unexpected divorce, and his now ex-wife took their precious daughter and moved 5-hours away, across the state. Before they moved, we lived just 15 minutes from them, and to my delight, I had gotten to see my first granddaughter regularly in her first year and a half.

That last day before the move, when my son brought her by so we could spend our last time together, was the last straw—the one I thought would break me into a million pieces. We had about an hour and half together before my son was also moving across the state just so he could stay near his daughter. My heart as a mom was breaking in two, watching my son go through this. And whatever might have been left of Mimi's heart was smashed into a million pieces.

It's one thing to have your own relationships broken. It's an entirely different thing to see your children go through difficult times. You would rather take the hit yourself than to ever watch them go through that kind of heart-wrenching pain. And every parent here said, AMEN!!

As I shut the door behind them and he loaded her into the car, the little bit of life remaining in me drained out completely. On top of all that, I watched our youngest son go through heartbreak of his own because my husband and I were on the verge of divorce.

Everywhere I turned, it seemed everyone was bleeding. And I was helpless to stop the hemorrhaging for any of us. Surely this is what King David in the Bible experienced at Ziklag when he was surrounded by complete devastation. Thank God for my church, a pastor who is a true shepherd and a handful of angel friends who stood by me through the good, the bad and the very ugly.

And very ugly it got as the weeks and months rolled on. I couldn't pour out my heart to my sister like I was used to. She needed me to stay positive and help her fight for her very life. So I would rally for her and my sons, and then lie down at night, wondering how I would ever be able to make it through the next day. Let me tell you, you find out quickly who your true friends are— the ones who will love you, stand in faith with you, let you cry, but not let you stay there! Pity parties are deadly, and thank God, no one ever let me throw one for very long or I never would have survived that year.

Loving friends who spoke gentle truth and didn't judge became as priceless diamonds to me. They would stand in faith with me on God's Word and pray fervent prayers with expectation that breakthroughs were in route. And by His grace, I ran *to* God and not away from Him. My heavenly Father put me under His "surgical knife" and lay my heart open for me to see it in His light during this season. It was not at all what I expected, but it was what was necessary, as it turned out.

Regardless of how much I thought my husband needed some "open heart surgery of his own," God said no. He was after what needed to be revealed and healed in me. Ouch! I can honestly say on this side, I'm grateful He gave me the grace to endure the process. You see, no matter how wrong someone else may have actually been or how much they hurt you, you are the only one you can fix. And when we submit to His process in our hearts, then we will be in a better place to pray godly prayers for those around us.

"Create in me a clean heart, O God; and renew a right spirit within me," (Psa. 51:10 KJV). I'll be honest with you. I was not happy with God in those moments of open heart surgery. After all, couldn't He see the absolute gut-wrenching pain I was in? He's a *loving* God, right? So what's up with this?

When He does this, what's up is: Love won't let you stay there if it's God's love. Love isn't always warm, mushy and comfortable. That's Hollywood's idea of love, not God's. So, don't let the devil convince you otherwise, for heaven's sake. Ole slew foot doesn't even know what love is! Who do you think has been selling Hollywood most of their scripts?

In the following weeks, all I could do was just focus on breathing, try to support my sons emotionally with what little I had left and desperately try to figure out how in the world a stay-at-home mom of some 20 years, who literally didn't even know how to turn on a computer, was going to make it at the age of 50, no less. Yikes, yikes and triple yikes! Was welfare around the corner? I had no job skills at this point that were desirable in the workforce.

Enter a couple of very dear sisters in the Lord and longtime friends who worked with me on the computer, showed me how to look for jobs and cheered me on! I didn't even have a way to repay them for all their love and support during that season. It was humbling to the core because I'm a giver at heart.

In the midst of all that and struggling to get back on my own two feet, I had prayerfully decided that I was going to stand, pray and believe for my marriage to be saved. Mind you, Lazarus had a better stinkin' chance of being raised from the dead than this marriage appeared to have! (Remember, laughter will take you a long way when storms hit!)

So I began a faith journey of praying and believing for restoration. Unbeknownst to me, at the very same time, our teenage son was loving on his dad via telephone and sharing whatever the Lord

laid on his heart to share with him. That in itself melted my heart—
that God's love and truth was so sweetly rooted in his heart and life.

Finances were an immediate concern, so I began looking
around for something to sell to help keep my son in the private,
Christian school he had known for so long. In my search for something with substantial worth, I decided to have a beautiful bronze
sculpture of Fredrick Remington's called "Coming Through the
Rye" appraised. My husband had given it to me for Christmas years
earlier, not long after I discovered and fell in love with it.

I chose well. It appraised high, and I found someone in Fort
Worth willing to give me $1,800 for it. Finally, a little good news!
It would pay for a few more months of school, and our son's routine
could remain stable in that area at least. I had it all planned out—
the day I would load it up and sell it. But while driving down a
familiar road, the Lord told me I needed to give that bronze as a
seed of faith, not only for our son's needs, but also for my marriage.

Listen, you have to be honest with God. He knows your
heart anyway, so I said, "Umm, in case you haven't noticed, tuition
is about due, and there is nothing to pay it with!"

To which He reassured me He was well aware of every
detail! But then He said something that would remain with me for
the rest of my life, "Precious seed will produce a precious harvest,
Lisa. And I not only know how much you love this sculpture, I
know how much you love and desire for your marriage to be
restored *and* for your son to be taken care of. I want you to sow this
and believe it will produce a precious harvest."

Now, as if that wasn't enough to rock my boat, He went on
to specifically tell me who to give it to. "What's wrong with that?
At least you now know who to give it to!" you might say.

Well, let me just put it this way. The name He gave me was the CEO of a large, worldwide ministry. Nice... Now God had me giving the last and most valuable thing I had left to the CEO of one of the largest ministries I was aware of, who probably wouldn't give me the time of day, even if I knew where he was or how to contact him. Talk about being humbled and laying down any sense of being a normal person. Now I was going to have to look like a nut! (Although, I'm sure this person had seen things like this before.)

Listen. When God's in something, and you're obedient to what He tells you to do, no matter how crazy it seems, the supernatural shows up every time! I picked up my phone and called one of my dear angel friends to talk this through. She picked up right away, and I told her what I just heard. When I finished, she excitedly said, "Yes, but not that person, his son." Great! Now my dear friend had gone wacky on me!

"What in the world are you talking about? This is crazy!!" I said.

"No, no. I know how you can get a hold of someone to see if he'll see you, and then you can give it to him."

Let me tell you, this whole thing got nuttier by the minute! She called me back shortly with the information I needed for an appointment. It just so happened, she used to be this person's assistant! Mind you, I had no idea that she had even worked in that position.

Long story short, God miraculously opened the door for me to meet this person and sow this precious seed. I shared the whole story, and he prayed for my precious harvest! Now here's the kicker.

God knows what He's doing, folks. When I gave the bronze to this man, the first thing he said was that his dad had the exact same one!

Yup.... It was supposed to go to him. And as it turned out, it looked like it was made for the table that would now be its home!

At this same time, the Lord began to reveal the power of first fruits to me: "Honor the Lord with your possessions, and with the first fruits of all your increase, so your barns will be filled with plenty and your vats will overflow with new wine," (Prov. 3:9-10). And He spoke to me about giving an offering at the beginning of the year at our church.

So again in faith, I gave and sowed the first of whatever I had, declaring that it would set the course of my year for miracles of all kinds. I trusted and knew His love for me was being established at a much deeper level than I had ever known in my walk with Him.

I'm glad I listened to God and glad I have friends that can hear God's voice. Sure enough, God supplied the tuition in supernatural ways after I sowed that seed. But most important of all, I got a phone call three and half months after planting that seed. My husband wanted to come home and restore the marriage if I was willing! That call was literally only a few short weeks before the final divorce decree. From there, God began to restore and straighten out the mess that we had made, and we had made a mess for sure!

But as I sit here, He has restored and keeps restoring, not only financially, but in every way! Just like the widow from the Bible with the last bit of oil, preparing to die with her son, we just keep getting the empty jars, and He keeps filling them all from that precious seed! God is able to restore anything to you. Just seek Him with all your heart, all your soul and all your strength, and He will lead you through and part the seas, if needed, for you to reach the other side!

Again, wherever you might find yourself in this moment, He can restore, heal, redeem and set you on your feet again. He loves you beyond what you can ever imagine, regardless of how messed up things may look. His plans for you are always good and always filled with more than you can ask or think. Give it completely to Him; rest in His faithfulness and in the power of His Word. When your faith reaches out and connects with the promises in the Word of God, there is spiritual power that takes over.

Call those things that be not as though they are (Rom. 4:17). See things with God's perspective and your spiritual eyes. *Everything, and I mean everything, is subject to change.* So only believe that God is able and more than willing to do the miraculous for you. Force your words to match God's words, and if you can't say anything positive and faith filled, say nothing at all. Your words are all the devil has to work with, so don't give him any ammunition. Instead, give him a migraine headache with the living Word of God!

Chapter Eight

MOVING FORWARD
TO DREAM AGAIN

A ll that you've just read is not even close to where the story ends. It's where it begins in a whole new and very unexpected way. We began to see miraculous restoration in our marriage and finances. I experienced the precious touch of healing in my heart as my sister went home to be with the Lord just eight months into our restored marriage. Her passing was a milestone in my life as she was my last living sibling and family member, other than my niece (her daughter).

As I write now, my niece, who had been in a nursing home for years due to mental and physical issues, passed away a little over a year and a half ago. But that is another story to be shared later. Honestly the emptiness from Sister passing was a chasm that felt as big as the Grand Canyon in my heart at times. Loss again drove me to my heavenly Father's lap and assurance from His Word that He would somehow mend my heart and begin to heal my soul. His perfect love for me preserved my soul, as Psalm 121 talks about, and taught me to enter His rest from the void and sorrow I felt at times like nothing else could. Having been through so much in a year's time, I felt certain that complete rest was what I needed.

Not so! Only three or four weeks after I returned from my sister's funeral and settling her estate, the Lord reminded me of a word and suggestion a friend at church had given me about going to work for a specific ministry. This friend and his wife and family had been friends of ours for years. And although I knew her to be very in tune with God, I wasn't really acquainted with him in that sense. Therefore, when he stopped me at a school function to share that he believed he heard as a very clear directive about this job, I was stunned and, in all honesty, dismissed it because it sounded so absurd. Absurd because I had no experience and no skills and was still a stay-at-home mom of 20-plus years.

Though it seemed ridiculous, I prayed because it was so out of the blue, and he shared it with such assuredness. Let me interject here that sometimes the Lord uses unusual avenues to get our attention, especially if it is something new He's trying to move us into! Just because it looks, sounds or appears completely foreign to what we would think, does not mean it might not be from God. Even though He is the Comforter, He likes to move us out of our self-imposed comfort zones and break us free from fear of any kind.

So as the Lord would have it, by faith I went forward and trusted Him. If He truly wanted me there, He would have to blow the door open, and open it did! And thus began a new chapter in my life, which has been amazing, challenging, stretching and something I would not trade for the world! God began to train me, and challenge me at every turn to come against my fears time and time again. The choice is always ours though. He will never impose His will upon you. Quitting is a choice that He will allow you to make, but rest assured that if you do, you will never know the blessing and dreams He had in store for you. It's been said, "If it was easy, everybody would do it." So true!

Not only was I trained in that position and began to conquer fear in a new way, I found something that I absolutely *loved* and knew was in my DNA to do! Nothing can compare to the knowing that comes from God that you've tapped into something He designed you to do from the foundation of your days and that you are able to bless others with. It doesn't matter what the actual job is, it's the fact that you have a portion and gifting from God to give back that is the blessing.

But know for sure, if it's something that seems over your head and beyond what you think you are capable of, there will be a battle with fear. Why wouldn't there be? Think about it, the enemy of your soul hates the thought that you can step out into something you're destined for and that requires faith in the one he hates—God.

Fear is a spirit, but God's Word says that God did not give us a spirit of fear. He has given us the ability to operate in power, love and a sound mind (2 Tim. 1:7). Although it may not be easy, you can definitely overcome fear. Besides, if it was easy, our flesh would try to take the credit, robbing God of all the glory!

If you remember anything from this book, remember this: Not only is there more for you, God wants you to ask, dream, stretch and keep growing, no matter your age. Young, old or in-between, you and I are not meant just to exist, couch sit and remain status quo!

This whole new chapter for me didn't start until the age of 50, and continues on now and beyond. Even if you are in your 70s,

80s and yes, even 90s, so what? It is not about what the world says we should be doing or not doing at these times in our lives, it's what the Word of God says! Psalm 91:16 says, *"With long life I will satisfy you and show you all of my salvation."* There is absolutely nothing that is impossible for God to do in and through your life, if you are open to it!

Now, if you are at all like I was, the concept of dreaming and seeing more for your life may be completely foreign or frozen by pain and fear. Sometimes we require healing and even counseling, if necessary, so we can re-adjust our sails to catch the wind to where God really wants to take us. If that's the case as it was for me, dare to step out and ask God, dream and start moving toward what you hear Him say.

In the past several years, the Lord made sure to surround me with anointed teachers and ministers who stretch my thinking, dreams and ideas in what the Lord says I can do. Terri Savelle Foy is one who helped resurrect my ability to dream and have vision for my life again. Through listening, reading and serving her, I began to give myself permission to dream and stretch for the future. Do not think you can do this without consistent reading, listening and walking out what God puts into your range of vision. If the Word of God says, "I can do all things through Christ who strengthens me," (Phil. 4:13) then I can, and so can you!

Chapter Nine

FAITH TO STRETCH

I t is truly all about the journey and not a destination as such. The destination shifts, changes and flows into the future all the time, whether you think it does or not. Time is moving, seasons are changing and life goes on, even if you don't move with it. Just go through your photo albums if you need confirmation on that one!

Even though that season and the job I had were amazing, stretching and God-given, it changed. And God told me after a couple of years, the season and the job were ending, and He needed me to do something else.

Now mind you, had He revealed the entire picture of what was around the corner, I'm sure I again would have thought there was absolutely no way I could enter into the next place of service and the position He wanted me to interview for. The initial instruction was simply to put in my notice and that I would be leaving. I had no idea where or what I would do next!

Again, I thought perhaps a season of eating bon-bons and resting for a while was at hand (hysterically laughing emoji here!). So when this opportunity came, I was stunned and hesitant once again because there were plenty of other candidates out there who were more experienced and more qualified than me. Just three weeks after leaving the first assignment, I interviewed and was hired! That set into motion the sale of our house and moving, and to where my husband and I would then begin to work!

A third shift, new jobs, and another move came just a year and a half after that for both of us, as only the Lord could do. The Lord sold homes and began to restore finances significantly in short periods of time through improving and flipping each home, and by sowing seeds.

The significance of sowing precious seed when the Holy Spirit prompts is vital for the harvest. To plant nothing and still expect a harvest doesn't work in the natural, so why would we ever expect it to work in the spiritual realm? The home that we are in now came into view when a prophet of God spoke in a message that I was listening to one day. He said to the women who had been believing for a dream house, their time was now!

When I heard that, it went off in me like an alarm! I took that word to heart, and I asked the Lord what seed to sow for this harvest of a dream home. Quickly, He showed how much and exactly where to give. Just five months later, we sold our home at a significant profit over what we had purchased it for just two years before, and we purchased a new home—lake view and all!

In only eight years, we literally went from being on the verge of divorce, having filed bankruptcy and both of us unemployed, to living in a beautiful home with a view of the lake and both of us working for one of the best ministries you could work for! ONLY GOD!

"And we know that all things work together for good to them that love God, to them who are called according to his purpose," (Rom. 8:28). This is truth. We have lived and seen it because we believed His love for us, and we loved His plan for us more than our own! We had not only tried our own plan and failed miserably, but we had never tasted and known the fullness of His love and grace for us.

Still, the journey and the stages and steps He wanted us to take were all choices. Neither of us had ever pictured or wanted to move as much as we have, but that was God's direction for us as He continued to restore, promote and get us to where we can serve for His kingdom purposes. We could have easily said, "No more; we're not moving again," and hindered what God was trying to do for and through us!

Let me say, the "things" in the natural take on a different meaning as you journey out of hard places. It's obvious from His Word that God wants to bless us, prosper us and give us all things to enjoy. The position these things hold in your heart shifts dramatically, allowing Him to even more fully bless you the way He wants to—exceedingly, abundantly above and beyond what we could ask or think (Eph. 3:20). Gratitude for His unfailing love far exceeds anything you could obtain in the natural. When you fully and truly continue to "Seek ye first the kingdom of God and his righteousness," then indeed, "all these things shall be added unto you" (Matt. 6:33 KJV). Gratitude abounds and becomes a way of life because nothing can compare to knowing and experiencing His love.

Even now, as I've picked back up this writing assignment to complete, God has transitioned me once again and had me retire from that wonderful job and come home by faith. I would love to be able to tell you He laid out a comprehensive plan and vision for this new season, but He didn't. It is becoming clear though that writing and whatever comes from that is what is next. It's really stretching me as it's not something I ever thought about doing. But apparently He has. Uncomfortable, scary and overwhelming are just a few of the top adjectives that describe this season. *But God...!*

I know beyond a shadow of a doubt I must step out in obedience and faith to fulfill what is quite possibly the very thing He saved me for from my mother's womb. As Terri Savelle Foy says, "There are people waiting on the other side of your obedience and mine to be healed and restored." This is eternal business—lives, souls at stake to hear and know that there is a very real Jesus who wants them healed and free so they can step into their own personal God assignments.

Chapter Ten

NOW IS THE TIME

D ivine order and restoration are always in God's heart for you and your life, regardless of how bad, chaotic or desolate it may look. That is the core of my entire testimony and life story I've shared. Whether you are slightly off course or don't even know where His path is for you, it's no more difficult for Him to restore, heal and drastically re-chart where you need to be, than it is to do a slight course correction! His love for you is so unfailing, merciful and generous that even if all you can do is stir up faith the size of a tiny mustard seed, He will begin to move, multiply and bless you.

God is love, and love desires to give. Really think about that in light of someone you love—your spouse, children, family. When you love them, even in the natural realm, you want to give them your time, gifts and encouragement. Then how much more does your heavenly Father want to give and do for you! "If you, then, though you are evil, know how to give good gifts to your children, how much more will your Father in heaven give good gifts to those who ask him!" (Matt. 7:11 NIV)

There is a key word within that verse that needs to be highlighted and brought to our attention. It's the word "ask." Let's look at Webster's definition of ask: *to call on for an answer; to seek information.* When we call, text or message someone we love, we expect to hear from them within a time frame that says, no matter how busy they are, they love and value us enough to respond as quickly as they can. Why should it be any different when we ask or inquire of the Lord? I really do believe that we make hearing from God way more difficult than it actually is or should be!

God loves us, He's not trying to keep information, encouragement or instruction from us; He's trying to get it to us. But first, we have to *ask.* Then we need to expect love will answer. Most of us who have spouses, children or close family know that, even though our day may be swamped, if one of our loved ones calls or texts, we will *make* the time to answer because of our love for them!

Your heavenly Father may be overseeing the entire universe, but I know His great and perfect love for us will draw Him to answer when we ask or inquire of Him. Therefore, ask and expect to hear from Him!

Begin to believe His love and receive that love just for you, no matter what your personal scenario is at this moment. Love never fails, and never means never! His is perfect love, not the kind Hollywood and romance novels depict. That's fantasy and has no validity or truth in it. The kind of love God is, is pure, never ending, unfailing and has no imperfections.

Now is the time to tap into all the love that God is and has for you. Once you truly grasp hold of that, everything will begin to change and move in the direction of all that God has for you and wants to accomplish through you. "NOW faith IS the substance of things hoped for, the evidence of things not seen," (Heb. 11:1 KJV).

His love will bring divine order and restoration even to the deepest, most difficult places in your heart and life, and He never slumbers or sleeps. The Lord wants to preserve, protect, bless and keep you in every area of your life. Today, tomorrow and forever more, He is in fact The Keeper!

Epilogue

My story and testimony has been unwrapped to share the hope of God's glory and love in my life and to reveal His love for you as well. It would not be complete unless I share here the *one* golden thread that runs through my story. I share it now with underscoring and highlighting, if you will, because if you don't see this, take this *and do it*, your breakthroughs and miracles will be hindered. It's such an important truth from God that it *must* be received, no matter how much you might think you can't or that it really doesn't matter. In fact, if you miss the revelation of this golden thread, then His power is limited, and not only is His power limited, but one day you will answer to why you haven't done this. So are you ready? Here it is...

FORGIVENESS!! "For if you forgive other people when they sin against you, your heavenly Father will also forgive you. But if you do not forgive others their sins, your Father will not forgive your sins," (Matt. 6:14-15 NIV).

These are strong, stout words from God. There are no exceptions or exemptions. None. Not one, no matter how painful, abusive or horrific the circumstances might have been in your life. There's no free pass because their sin and treatment was beyond what any human should ever suffer. Believe me, I can just hear some of you saying, "Listen here. You have no idea what I have suffered through!"

You are right in the sense that I may not know what the actual circumstances are. *But* what I absolutely do know is that Jesus has already suffered and died far beyond what we can wrap our brains around, so we can forgive. We *must* forgive as He did.

Jesus hung on that cross and endured every sin that the human race would ever commit and every demonic force we would ever know. *Yet* He said, "Father, forgive them; for they know not what they do," (Luke 23:34 KJV). If Jesus was required to forgive, what makes us think we aren't? The fact is, heaven is a place where no sickness, sin or unforgiveness can dwell. Heaven is a place of joy, wholeness and peace and was built on the very foundation of forgiveness for *us* through the precious gift of God's only Son, Jesus Christ. Oh, the mercy, grace and love of God for us is so very wide and deep and broad.

Well, you might say, "Where was God when…?" and you fill in that blank. He was right there, my friend. It was not His will for you to be hurt, abused or misused, but man has free will, and the enemy roams this earth as a roaring lion, seeking whom he may devour (1 Pet. 5:8). Fact is, it's as simple as this: God is GOOD and the devil is BAD. And should you not believe that there really is a devil or a viable spirit realm, just turn on the news and look at the absolute evil being reported on a daily basis.

The Bible tells us, "For we wrestle not against flesh and blood, but against principalities, against powers, against the rulers of the darkness of this world, against spiritual wickedness in high places," (Eph. 6:12 KJV). Who do you think is seeking to keep you in the past with all that pain and bitterness in your soul? The devil loves it when he can imprison people in pain and unforgiveness. It keeps them from freedom and heaven.

Now mind you, that does not make right or condone in any way what happened to you or negate the pain. The forgiveness we give is primarily for *us*! Forgiveness also doesn't mean that you have to allow people's unhealthy or dangerous behaviors into your inner circle. God wants us to learn healthy relationships and boundaries. Not everyone is supposed to be your best friend. However, when we can forgive others of our own free will, then not only does freedom and healing come for us, but then we can begin to really pray for those that have hurt us. Remember, as Joyce Meyer so succinctly put it, "Hurt people hurt people."

So as we say goodbye, my prayer is that right where you are, you would go to your heavenly Father with your pain and unforgiveness, and ask Him to help you forgive certain people in your life. And while you're at it, don't forget this important key: to forgive yourself as well for any self-inflicted wounds you may have. Let the tears flow. Share your innermost pain and disappointments with Him, and watch His Love absolutely infiltrate your heart, mind and soul.

He *loves you* so very much, and He alone is the only one who can heal the impossible and help you forgive the inexcusable. God is the answer. He is the missing piece to your hurt or empty life. And He is, dear one, *The Keeper* of your life!

Prayer for Salvation and
Baptism in the Holy Spirit

_____

I f you've read this book and know that you in fact need Jesus, this is for you at this very moment in time. It's not a mistake or an accident that this book has come into your hands.

The Jesus that I shared about in my life wants desperately to be in yours. So much so that had you been the only one on the face of this earth, He would have died on that cross just for YOU!

The fact is there is an eternity, and there is a choice: heaven with Him or hell. It's your choice that will determine how you will spend eternity.

So if you know that you haven't repented of your sins and asked Jesus Christ into your heart, and you've felt a tugging, a nudging throughout this book, then answer that call, and pray this prayer for salvation and the infilling of the Holy Spirit:

"Dear Lord Jesus, I humbly come before you now and repent of my sins and ask for your forgiveness. Thank you, Jesus, that you loved me so much that you took my place at the cross and paid for those sins in full. Your Word says, 'Whosoever shall call on the name of the Lord shall be saved,' (Acts 2:21 KJV). I ask now that you come into my heart and life as my Savior and Lord, and from this day forward, I will serve you and follow you. It also says in Your Word, 'If ye then, being evil, know how to give good gifts unto your children: how much more shall your heavenly Father give the Holy Spirit to them that ask him?' (Luke 11:13) Therefore,

I'm also asking You to fill me now with the Holy Spirit. In fact, I'm expecting to speak with other tongues as you begin to pour forth through me (Acts 2:4). In Jesus' name, amen!"

Begin to thank and praise Him for the best decision you've ever made in your life! Then ask Him to show you the church you need to become a part of where you can begin to grow in Him and have faith-filled friends surround you in your new life. It's so vitally important that you're connected with a solid church that teaches the Bible and moves in the Holy Spirit.

Forgiving Others and
Healing Your Heart

Our God is amazing, and He is able to help you forgive others and begin the process of healing your heart. If there are those in your life that you know you need to forgive, just pray the following prayer as your own:

"Right now, Father, as an act of my will, I choose to forgive the following people who have wounded or hurt me: (fill in the blank with their names here). Your Word says, 'For if you forgive men their trespasses, your heavenly Father will also forgive you. But if you do not forgive men their trespasses, neither will your Father forgive your trespasses,' (Matt. 6:14-15). Thank you, Father, that my forgiveness isn't based on how I feel. Feelings change, but this is an act of my will and in obedience to what your Word says.

"Now Father, I thank you for your healing power to come into my heart. All the brokenness and pain I give to You. For it says in Psalms 147:3, 'He heals the brokenhearted and binds up their wounds.' Thank you, Lord, for the peace and healing that is flooding old memories and abuses to my body, spirit and emotions. All things are becoming new, and I know the plans You have for me are for good," (Jer. 29:11). In the name of Jesus, amen."

About the Author

LISA MANASCO is a wife, mother and Mimi first and foremost. She and her husband live near Dallas, Texas, and have been married 32 years and counting. Put her in a leopard-print prayer chair with a hot cup of coffee and let her talk about Jesus, and you have captured the DNA of who she is! Lisa's desire is to see those who don't yet know Jesus come into a living, thriving relationship with Him, to see the hurting healed and to see those who are in bondage freed from any and all life-hindering circumstances.